United States Government Accountability Office

Report to the Chairman, Subcommittee on Social Security, Committee on Ways and Means, House of Representatives

May 2013

SOCIAL SECURITY ADMINISTRATION

Long-Term Strategy Needed to Address Key Management Challenges

I0448368

GAO Highlights

Highlights of GAO-13-459, a report to the Chairman, Subcommittee on Social Security, Committee on Ways and Means, House of Representatives

SOCIAL SECURITY ADMINISTRATION

Long-Term Strategy Needed to Address Key Management Challenges

Why GAO Did This Study

SSA is responsible for providing benefits and services that affect the lives of nearly every American. In calendar year 2012, SSA paid over 62 million people more than $826 billion in Social Security retirement and disability benefits and Supplemental Security Income payments. However, SSA faces increased workloads and large numbers of potential employee retirements in the long term. It is expected that a new Commissioner will soon be leading the agency. GAO was asked to describe issues confronting SSA. This report examines (1) key management challenges SSA faces in meeting its mission-related objectives, and (2) the extent to which SSA's planning efforts address these challenges. To do this, GAO reviewed relevant planning documents and reports from SSA and others as well as SSA management information and data on workload and staffing projections, and applicable federal laws and regulations; and interviewed SSA headquarters and regional officials, representatives of employee groups, and other experts.

What GAO Recommends

To address SSA's key management challenges, the agency should (1) consider having an entity or individual dedicated to strategic planning, (2) develop a long-term strategy for service delivery, (3) take steps to update its succession plan, and (4) explore the utility and feasibility of realigning its headquarters, regional, and field office structure. SSA agreed with our recommendations and outlined plans for implementation.

View GAO-13-459. For more information, contact Daniel Bertoni at (202) 512-7215 or bertonid@gao.gov

What GAO Found

The Social Security Administration (SSA) will experience management challenges in four key areas over the next decade.

Human capital. SSA has not updated its succession plan since 2006 although the agency faces an ongoing retirement wave and hiring freeze which will make it difficult to respond to growing workload demands.

Disability program issues. SSA faces ongoing challenges incorporating a more modern concept of disability into its programs, while balancing competing needs to reduce backlogs of initial and appealed claims and ensure program integrity.

Information technology (IT). SSA has made strides in modernizing its IT systems to address growing workload demands, but faces challenges with these modernization efforts and correcting internal weaknesses in information security.

Physical infrastructure. SSA is moving toward centralized facilities management, but the agency lacks a proactive approach to evaluating its office structure that will identify potential efficiencies, such as consolidating offices.

Long-Term Projected Growth in SSA's Workload Coincides with Large Numbers of Potential Employee Retirements

Source: GAO analysis of SSA beneficiary data from the 2012 Annual Report of the Board of Trustees of the Federal Old-Age and Survivors Insurance and Federal Disability Insurance Trust Funds and the 2012 Annual Report of the Supplemental Security Income Program and projected retirement data extracted from the Human Resources Operational Data Store.

SSA has ongoing planning efforts, but they do not address the long-term nature of these management challenges. For example, SSA is finalizing a service delivery plan, but it only includes detailed plans for the next 5 years and focuses on existing initiatives rather than articulating specific long-term strategies for the agency's service delivery model. Its current strategic plan also largely describes the continuation, expansion, or enhancement of ongoing activities, rather than proposing broad changes to address emerging issues. Since 2008, SSA has not had an entity or individual dedicated to strategic planning. Various groups have called on SSA to articulate a longer-term strategy, which it last did in 2000, motivated by many conditions which remain true today—such as increasing workloads, advances in technology, and employee retirements—and which will need to be addressed in the future. Strategic planning literature and experts cite key long-term planning practices such as planning for different scenarios and aligning interim plans with the long-term strategy as necessary for success.

_____ United States Government Accountability Office

Contents

Abbreviations

CDR	continuing disability reviews
CIO	Chief Information Officer
COBOL	Common Business Oriented Language
DDS	Disability Determination Services
DI	Disability Insurance
FISMA	Federal Information Security Management Act of 2002
GSA	General Services Administration
GPRA	Government Performance and Results Act
IT	information technology
O*NET	Occupational Information Network
OASI	Old-Age and Survivors Insurance
OFSM	SSA's Office of Facilities and Supply Management
OIG	SSA's Office of the Inspector General
OMB	Office of Management and Budget
RRB	Railroad Retirement Board
SNAP	Supplemental Nutrition Assistance Program
SSA	Social Security Administration
SSI	Supplemental Security Income

GAO

U.S. GOVERNMENT ACCOUNTABILITY OFFICE

441 G St. N.W.
Washington, DC 20548

May 29, 2013

The Honorable Sam Johnson
Chairman
Subcommittee on Social Security
Committee on Ways and Means
House of Representatives

Dear Mr. Chairman:

The Social Security Administration (SSA) is responsible for providing benefits and services that affect the lives of nearly every American. In calendar year 2012, SSA paid over 62 million people more than $826 billion in Social Security retirement and disability benefits and Supplemental Security Income payments. As more members of the baby boom generation become eligible for retirement benefits and individuals under age 62 reach their disability-prone years, a surge in benefit applications is expected. Evolving technology will affect service delivery expectations, and SSA's own workforce may also change and decrease in the coming years. At the same time, SSA's expanded use of electronic services will affect how the agency should deploy and use its workforce. In addition, the agency will need to operationalize any legislative changes that may be made in an effort to avoid the projected exhaustion of the Social Security trust funds. As a result of these realities, SSA will encounter increased pressure to serve the public while still ensuring program integrity. Moreover, SSA will likely continue to experience budget constraints.

A new Commissioner will soon be leading the agency and will face these many interrelated issues.[1] Decisions made early in the Commissioner's term could help set the course for the agency over the long term and determine how well-positioned it is to adapt to changing realities.[2] GAO was asked to describe issues confronting SSA. This report addresses (1)

---

[1]The SSA Commissioner is appointed for a 6-year term. 42 U.S.C. § 902(a)(3). The last Commissioner's term expired on January 19, 2013, and an acting commissioner is currently leading the agency. As of May 2013, a new Commissioner had not yet been appointed.

[2]In this report, when referring to short-term, we generally mean up to 5 years out and by long-term we mean more than 5 years.

GAO-13-459 SSA Management Challenges

key management challenges SSA faces in meeting its mission-related objectives and (2) the extent to which SSA's planning efforts address these challenges.

To examine these issues, we obtained SSA management information and administrative data related to workload and staffing projections. We assessed the reliability of the data by reviewing related documentation and interviewing knowledgeable agency officials and determined they were sufficiently reliable to describe agency projections. We also reviewed key agency planning and other documents, such as SSA's strategic plan, strategic human capital plan, strategic leadership succession plan, information technology strategic plan, facilities standards, and agency-wide draft service delivery plan. We conducted in-depth interviews with SSA officials, including regional commissioners, and other experts, including representatives of the Social Security Advisory Board and others familiar with long-term planning. We reviewed GAO internal control standards and relevant GAO, SSA Office of the Inspector General (OIG), and Social Security Advisory Board reports, as well as applicable federal laws and regulations and SSA's policies and procedures.[3] See appendix I for more on our scope and methodology.

We conducted this performance audit from September 2012 to May 2013 in accordance with generally accepted government auditing standards. Those standards require that we plan and perform the audit to obtain sufficient, appropriate evidence to provide a reasonable basis for our findings and conclusions based on our audit objectives. We believe that the evidence obtained provides a reasonable basis for our findings and conclusions based on our audit objectives.

Background

SSA provides financial assistance to eligible individuals through three major benefit programs:

- Old-Age and Survivors Insurance (OASI)—provides retirement benefits to older workers and their families and to survivors of deceased workers.

---

[3]For relevant prior GAO work on this topic, see the Related GAO Products list.

- Disability Insurance (DI)—provides benefits to eligible workers who have qualifying disabilities, and their eligible family members.

- Supplemental Security Income (SSI)—provides income for aged, blind, or disabled individuals with limited income and resources.

SSA projects that the number of beneficiaries and benefit payments for the three programs will increase over the next several years (see figures 1 and 2). DI and SSI are the nation's largest federal disability programs, and applications for benefits have grown significantly over the last 5 years, due in part to baby boomers reaching their disability-prone years, as well as a sustained economic downturn and high unemployment. Retirement claims have also steadily increased in recent years.

Figure 1: Beneficiaries of Old-Age and Survivors Insurance, Disability Insurance, and Supplemental Security Income Programs in Payment Status as of the End of the Year

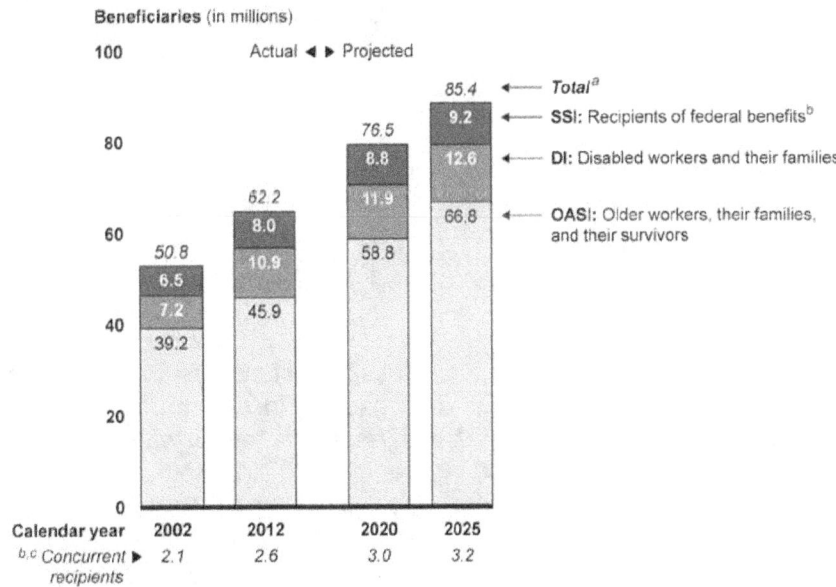

Source: GAO analysis of SSA data from the 2012 Annual Report of the Board of Trustees of the Federal Old-Age and Survivors Insurance and Federal Disability Insurance Trust Funds; and the 2012 Annual Report of the Supplemental Security Income Program.

[a]The total refers to the number of individuals with either an OASI, DI, or federal SSI benefit. Concurrent beneficiaries are excluded from the total to avoid double-counting.

[b]According to SSA, some individuals are ineligible for federal SSI benefits due to excess income, but are eligible for State supplementation. These individuals are not included in these recipient counts.

[c]Concurrent recipients are those receiving federal SSI benefits and benefits from either the OASI or DI program. These figures are included in the OASI, DI, and SSI counts above.

GAO-13-459 SSA Management Challenges

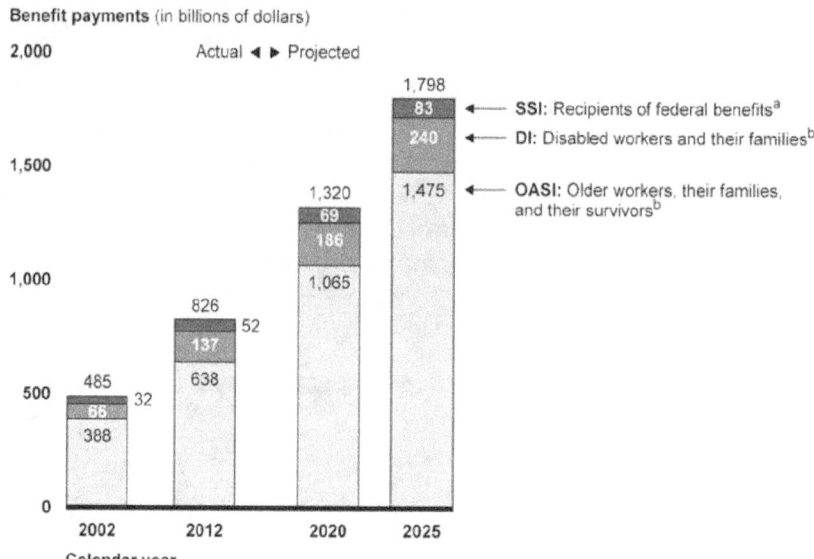

Figure 2: Federal Benefit Outlays for Old-Age and Survivors Insurance, Disability Insurance, and Supplemental Security Income Programs

Benefit payments (in billions of dollars)

Actual ◄ ► Projected

SSI: Recipients of federal benefits[a]

DI: Disabled workers and their families[b]

OASI: Older workers, their families, and their survivors[b]

Calendar year

Source: GAO analysis of SSA data from the 2012 Annual Report of the Board of Trustees of the Federal Old-Age and Survivors Insurance and Federal Disability Insurance Trust Funds and the 2012 Annual Report of the Supplemental Security Income Program.

[a]This figure includes federal SSI outlays only. It excludes state supplementation benefits. Federal SSI outlays reflect actual timing of payments. For any calendar year, outlays exclude payments due on January 1 of the given year but include payments due on January 1 of the following year.

[b]This figure includes an offset for reimbursements due to un-negotiated checks and payments to providers of vocational rehabilitation services.

Although SSA's disability programs account for only about 23 percent of its total benefit outlays, they represent 66 percent of the administrative expenses for these 3 programs (see fig. 3). Complex eligibility rules and many layers of review with multiple handoffs from one person to another make the disability programs complicated, and therefore costly, to administer. After the field office determines that an applicant has met SSA's nonmedical eligibility requirements for disability benefits,[4] the applicant's claim is sent to the state Disability Determination Services

---

[4]For example, SSA will ensure that an SSI applicant meets income requirements and determine if a DI applicant has a sufficient work history.

(DDS) for a review of the claimant's medical eligibility.[5] After assembling all medical and vocational information for the claim, a DDS examiner in consultation with appropriate medical staff determines whether the claimant meets the requirements of the law for having a disability. Claimants who are dissatisfied with the initial DDS determination have up to three levels of appeal, including a "reconsideration" of the claim, conducted by DDS personnel who were not involved in the original decision; a hearing before an administrative law judge; and a review of the claim by the Appeals Council, which is comprised of administrative appeals judges and appeals officers.

Figure 3: Administrative Expenses for Old-Age and Survivors Insurance, Disability Insurance, and Supplemental Security Income Programs in Fiscal Year 2012

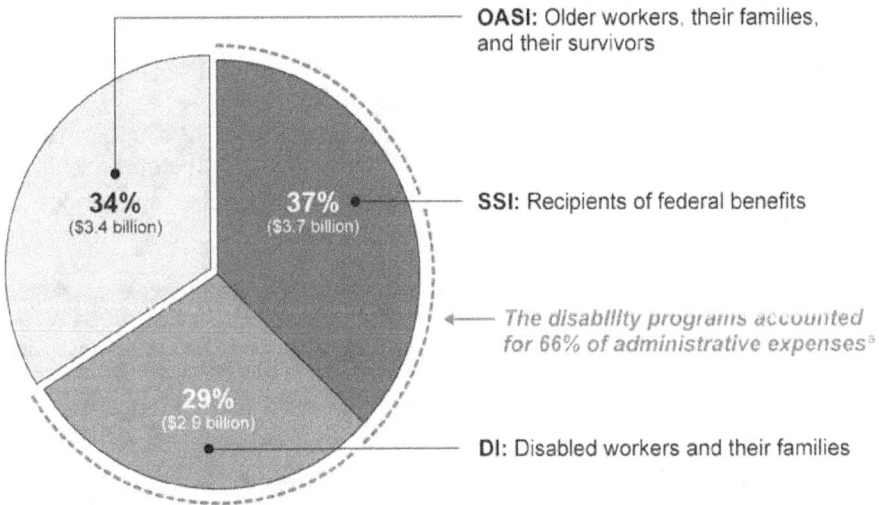

OASI: Older workers, their families, and their survivors

SSI: Recipients of federal benefits

The disability programs accounted for 66% of administrative expenses[a]

DI: Disabled workers and their families

Source: GAO analysis of data from SSA's Office of Budget.

[a]Administrative expenses such as personnel and physical infrastructure associated with OASI, DI and SSI programs account for approximately 86 percent of the agency's total administrative budget. Other administrative expenses not associated with programs include research and operations for SSA's Office of the Inspector General.

[5]SSA generally considers individuals disabled if they cannot do work that they did before; they cannot adjust to other work because of their medical condition(s); and their disability has lasted or is expected to last for at least 1 year or to result in death. See 42 U.S.C. § 423(d). Although SSA is responsible for the program, the law generally calls for initial determinations of disability to be made by state DDS agencies. See 42 U.S.C. § 421(a)(1).The work performed at DDS offices is federally financed and carried out under SSA disability program regulations, policies, and guidelines.

Both OASI and DI face long-term financial challenges. SSA's Office of the Chief Actuary has reported that OASI cannot sustain projected long-run program costs under currently scheduled financing, and that legislative modifications are necessary to avoid disruptive consequences for beneficiaries and taxpayers. In 2012, SSA's Office of the Chief Actuary projected that the DI and OASI Trust Funds would be exhausted in 2016 and 2035, respectively. If the trust funds are depleted before legislative changes are made to restore long-term solvency, the agency projects that it will be able to pay benefits only to the extent that funds are available.[6]

In support of its mission and programs, SSA's basic functions include maintaining earnings information, making initial eligibility determinations for program payments, making changes to beneficiaries' accounts that affect their benefit payments, and issuing Social Security numbers.[7] SSA also provides administrative support to the Medicare program, partners with the Department of Homeland Security in verifying employment eligibility for new hires, and assists with the administration of other programs, such as the Supplemental Nutrition Assistance Program (SNAP) and Railroad Retirement Board (RRB) benefits program.[8] Table 1 includes volume data on some key aspects of SSA's workload for fiscal year 2012.

Table 1: Selected Aspects of SSA's Workload and Volume, Fiscal Year 2012

Maintaining earnings information	
Earnings items posted to workers' records	220 million
Making initial eligibility determinations for program payments	
Retirement, survivor, and Medicare applications received	5 million
Initial disability applications received	3.2 million
Denied disability applications reconsidered	809,000
Hearings conducted	672,000
Appeals Council reviews completed	166,000

[6]While money would still be coming in from the Social Security taxes paid by current workers, the agency projects that it would not be sufficient for beneficiaries to receive their full benefit.

[7]Social Security numbers have become the universal identifier of choice for government agencies and are currently used for many non-Social Security purposes.

[8]SSA offices take applications for SNAP and certify Social Security benefits for the RRB.

GAO-13-459 SSA Management Challenges

Making changes to beneficiaries' accounts that affect benefit payments	
Overpayment actions completed	3.2 million
SSI non-disability redeterminations completed	2.6 million
Continuing disability reviews completed	443,000
Issuing Social Security numbers	
New and replacement Social Security cards issued	16 million
Other functions	
Automated Social Security number verifications performed	1.5 billion
Transactions completed on National 800 Number	56 million
Visitors assisted	45 million

Source: GAO analysis of SSA data from SSA's FY 2012 Performance Accountability Report.

SSA has over 80,000 state and federal employees[9] to administer SSA programs in about 1,700 facilities nationwide. These facilities include regional offices, field offices, teleservice centers, processing centers, hearings offices, the Appeals Council, and SSA's headquarters in Baltimore, Maryland. Almost 182,000 people visit one of the nearly 1,300 SSA field offices daily, and more than 445,000 people call the offices daily to file applications, ask questions, or update their information.

SSA is operating in an environment of constrained resources and budgetary uncertainty. According to a former SSA commissioner and agency budget documents, while SSA's administrative budget increased about 32 percent from fiscal year 2001 to 2010,[10] much of this funding has been used to keep up with increases in expenses such as personnel costs, rent, and security. Furthermore, for several years Congress has passed continuing resolutions to prevent funding gaps when regular appropriations bills have not been enacted by the start of a fiscal year. As we have previously reported, operating under a continuing resolution may limit agencies' management options and lead to incremental planning and repetitive activities, resulting in inefficiencies.[11]

---

[9]SSA funds DDSs, which are state agencies, to process disability applications and conduct continuing disability reviews in accordance with SSA policies and procedures.

[10]This figure has been adjusted for inflation. The nominal increase between fiscal years 2001 and 2010 was about 61 percent.

[11]GAO, *Continuing Resolutions: Uncertainty Limited Management Options and Increased Workload in Selected Agencies*, GAO-09-879 (Washington, D.C.: September 24, 2009).

GAO-13-459 SSA Management Challenges

SSA Faces Key Management Challenges in Human Capital, Disability Program Issues, Information Technology, and Physical Infrastructure

Over the next decade, SSA will experience management challenges in four key areas: 1) human capital, 2) disability program issues, 3) information technology, and 4) physical infrastructure.

SSA's Strategies to Prevent a Leadership and Skills Shortage May Be Insufficient During a Time of Increasing Workloads

Over the next decade SSA's ongoing retirement wave, coupled with a hiring freeze that has been in place since 2010, will create significant management challenges for the agency in meeting its projected growth in work demands. Although not all employees will necessarily retire when eligible, nearly 7,000 headquarters employees and more than 24,000 field employees will become retirement eligible between 2011 and 2020. The agency projects that it could lose nearly 22,500 employees, or nearly one-third of its workforce, during this time due to retirement—its primary source of attrition (see fig. 4).[12] Officials told us that as a result of the hiring freeze, they have been unable to back-fill positions vacated by retiring employees. The Commissioner stated in SSA's fiscal year 2012 budget overview that as a result of attrition, some offices could become understaffed, and that without a sufficient number of skilled employees, backlogs and wait times could significantly increase and improper payments could grow. As SSA's workforce decreases and its workload increases, the agency's strategies for preventing a loss of leadership and skills may prove insufficient for a variety of reasons.

---

[12]Data reflect SSA's most recent projections from its September 2011 Retirement Wave Report, which only includes actual retirement figures through fiscal year 2010. Officials told us that they previously produced this report annually but currently produce it every other year.

Figure 4: Actual and Projected Retirements of SSA Staff, Fiscal Years 2009-2020

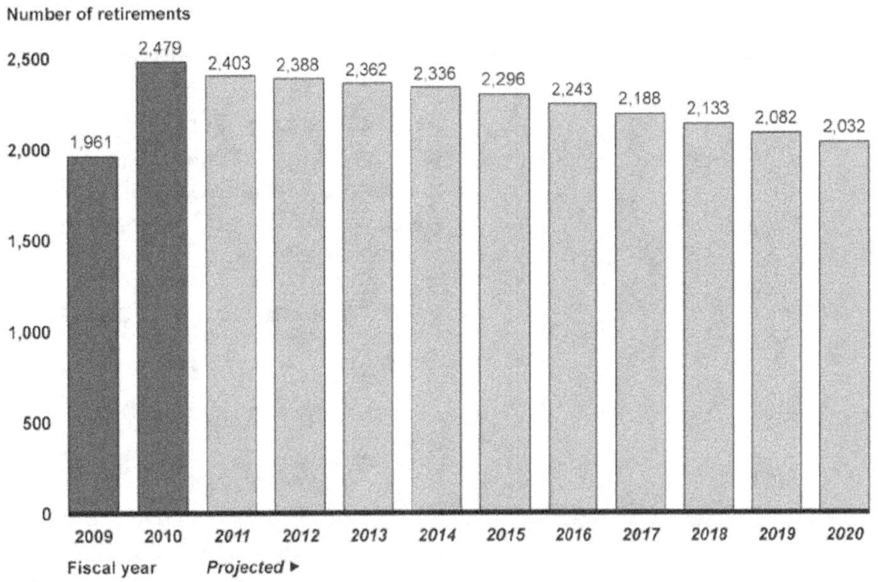

Number of retirements

Fiscal year	Number of retirements
2009	1,961
2010	2,479
2011	2,403
2012	2,388
2013	2,362
2014	2,336
2015	2,296
2016	2,243
2017	2,188
2018	2,133
2019	2,082
2020	2,032

Fiscal year   Projected ►

Source: GAO analysis of SSA data extracted from the Human Resources Operational Data Store.

Note: Numbers refer to retirements of full-time and part-time permanent employees. Data reflect SSA's most recent projections from its September 2011 Retirement Wave Report, which only includes actual retirement figures through fiscal year 2010.

Retaining institutional knowledge and developing new leaders. SSA could face a significant loss of institutional knowledge and expertise in the coming years. An estimated 43 percent of SSA's non-supervisory employees and 60 percent of its supervisors will be eligible to retire by 2020 (see fig. 5). The high percentage of supervisors who are eligible to retire could leave a gap in terms of certain skills or institutional knowledge. For example, regional and district managers told us they have lost staff experienced in handling the most complex disability cases and providing guidance on policy compliance.[13] SSA officials and DDS managers told us that it typically takes 2 to 3 years for new employees to become fully proficient and that new hires benefit from mentoring by veteran employees. Because of budget cutbacks, SSA has also curtailed its leadership development programs, which have historically been used to establish a pipeline of future leaders. According to SSA officials, the

---

[13]According to SSA, DDS staff are state employees and are subject to state furloughs.

GAO-13-459 SSA Management Challenges

pressure to keep up with workload demands in the face of staff losses and the loss of leadership development programs will likely negatively affect employee morale. Some officials also said low morale and a feeling of being stretched too thin are hastening retirement among those who are eligible. Employees rated the agency lower on the Office of Personnel Management's Federal Employee Viewpoint Survey in 2012 than in 2011 in terms of the extent to which they think the agency has the talent necessary to achieve organizational goals (59 percent compared to 62 percent) and the extent to which they are satisfied with their jobs (68 percent compared to 72 percent).[14]

Figure 5: Percentage of Non-Supervisors and Supervisors at SSA Eligible for Retirement, Fiscal Years 2011–2020

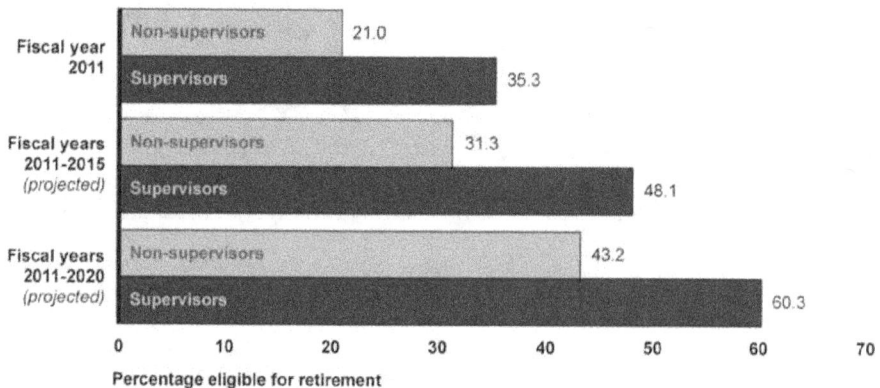

Percentage eligible for retirement

Source: GAO analysis of SSA data extracted from the Human Resources Operational Data Store.

Note: Numbers refer to retirements of full-time and part-time permanent employees. Eligibility figures are cumulative.

Succession planning. SSA's most recent succession plan was issued in 2006, even though the agency has experienced significant changes since that time, including a hiring freeze and greater movement toward online

---

[14]The Federal Employee Viewpoint Survey is a tool that measures employees' perceptions of whether, and to what extent, conditions that characterize successful organizations are present in their agencies. Agency results have a margin of error of less than plus or minus 1 percentage point. Data collected from survey respondents were weighted to produce estimates that represent the agency population. Office of Personnel Management, *2012 Federal Employee Viewpoint Survey Results: Employees Influencing Change, Governmentwide Management Report.* (Washington, D.C.).

services. The most recent succession plan established a target of evaluating and updating the plan by the end of 2007. GAO's *Standards for Internal Control in the Federal Government* state that management should ensure that skill needs are continually assessed and that the organization is able to obtain a workforce with those required skills to achieve organizational goals.[15] GAO's internal controls guidance also states that management should consider how best to retain valuable employees, plan for their eventual succession, and ensure continuity of needed skills and abilities. Leading organizations use succession planning to identify, develop, and select successors who are the right people, with the right skills, at the right time for leadership and other key positions.[16] Other key principles of strategic workforce planning include determining critical skills and competencies that will be needed to achieve current and future programmatic results and developing strategies to address gaps in these skills and competencies.[17]

SSA's 2006 succession plan states that without sound succession planning, SSA's loss of leadership would result in a drain on institutional knowledge and expertise at a time when workloads are growing. This loss of knowledge and expertise could result in increasing workloads, backlogs, and improper payments. Several SSA officials told us the lack of proper succession planning can be detrimental to future agency operations. For example, they said individuals with less experience and training are beginning to assume supervisory roles and some have made poor decisions related to such things as employee contract issues and providing reasonable accommodations to employees with disabilities. Some officials also told us that inexperienced managers are less proficient at supervising others, which leads to inefficiencies in managing

---

[15]GAO, *Standards for Internal Control in the Federal Government*, GAO/AIMD-00-21.3.1 (Washington, D.C.: November 1, 1999).

[16]See GAO, *Human Capital: Succession Planning and Management Is Critical Driver of Organizational Transformation*, GAO-04-127T (Washington, D.C.: October 1, 2003) and GAO, *Human Capital: Selected Agencies Have Opportunities to Enhance Existing Succession Planning and Management Efforts*, GAO-05-585 (Washington, D.C.: June 30, 2005).

[17]Strategic workforce planning addresses two critical needs: (1) aligning an organization's human capital program with its current and emerging mission and programmatic goals and (2) developing long-term strategies for acquiring, developing, and retaining staff to achieve programmatic goals. GAO, *Human Capital: Key Principles for Effective Strategic Workforce Planning*, GAO-04-39 (Washington, D.C.: December 11, 2003).

increasing workloads. Moreover, SSA employees' perceptions of agency leaders' ability to motivate staff, communicate goals and priorities, and demonstrate other leadership behaviors diminished from 2011 to 2012 among those responding to the Office of Personnel Management's Federal Employee Viewpoint Survey.[18]

SSA's Strategic Human Capital Plan does not establish an explicit requirement for how frequently the agency will update its succession plan, but it identifies the succession plan as one component for determining how SSA makes data-driven decisions to continuously improve the agency's human capital practices. Senior SSA officials told us that the agency's succession plan has not been updated more recently because the analyst staff who were responsible for preparing it have been reassigned to other duties that the agency considered more urgent, such as managing personnel programs. SSA officials also noted that in the current budgetary environment, conducting succession planning has become a luxury.

Forecasting workforce needs. Findings from OIG reports raise additional concerns about SSA's ability to accurately forecast workload demands and workforce needs.[19] These reports found methodological flaws in the workload and work year data SSA uses to formulate and execute its budget. For example, the reports concluded that the internal controls and main processes related to work sampling—which SSA uses to measure work and assign direct and indirect costs to workloads—did not ensure the completeness and reliability of data in SSA's Cost Analysis System.[20] The reports found that work samples were not consistently

---

[18]In response to a combination of questions designed to assess employee's perceptions of the integrity of leadership, as well as leadership behaviors such as communication and workforce motivation, 66 percent of SSA employees had a favorable view of agency leadership in 2011, compared to 62 percent of employees in 2012.

[19]SSA's OIG contracted with Grant Thornton LLP to conduct the following reviews of SSA's Cost Analysis System and cost allocation methodology: SSA OIG, *Cost Analysis System Background Report and Viability Assessment*, A-15-10-20149 (April 20, 2011); SSA OIG, *Office of Disability Adjudication and Review Cost Allocation Process*, A-15-10-20150 (May 5, 2011); SSA OIG, *The Social Security Administration Cost Allocation Process*, A-15-10-20151 (Dec. 7, 2011); and SSA OIG, *The Social Security Administration Cost Allocation Methodology*, A-15-10-20152 (June 18, 2012).

[20]SSA's Cost Analysis System is used to allocate (1) administrative costs to Trust Fund and general fund programs administered by SSA and (2) reimbursable work performed by SSA for outside organizations.

performed. Furthermore, they noted no instances of peer or management review, which could improve the accuracy of the workload data collected.[21] SSA is taking steps to improve data sampling in response to these findings.

SSA Continues to Face Challenges in Modernizing Its Disability Programs, While Seeking a Balance Between Reducing Backlogs and Ensuring Program Integrity

Modernizing disability programs. We designated federal disability programs as a high-risk area in 2003, in part because these programs emphasize medical conditions in assessing an individual's work incapacity without adequate consideration of the work opportunities afforded by advances in medicine, technology, and job demands.[22] Concerns have been raised that the medical listings being used lack current and relevant criteria to evaluate disability applicants' inability to work, and that by failing to consider the role of assistive devices, and workplace accommodations, SSA may be missing opportunities to help individuals with disabilities return to work. In 2012, we noted that resource constraints have impeded SSA's efforts to ensure timely updates to its medical criteria.[23] However, SSA has recently taken steps toward comprehensively updating the medical and labor market information that underlie its disability criteria. As of March 2013, SSA had completed comprehensive revisions of its medical criteria for 10 of the 14 adult body systems and initiated targeted reviews of certain conditions under these systems, as appropriate, according to SSA officials.[24]

SSA has also recently made progress toward replacing its outdated occupational information system, including signing an interagency

---

[21]SSA officials told us that these data are statistically reliable at a national level and are combined with other data sources to forecast workloads. However, SSA has not yet assessed enough work sampling data to produce a refined estimate of the statistical reliability of workload calculations based on work sampling data.

[22]GAO, *High-Risk Series: An Update*, GAO-13-283 (Washington, D.C.: February 14, 2013).

[23]GAO, *Modernizing SSA Disability Programs: Progress Made, but Key Efforts Warrant More Management Focus*, GAO-12-420 (Washington, D.C.: June 19, 2012).

[24]To determine an applicant's eligibility for disability benefits, SSA examiners assess the applicant's medical impairments against the Listings of Impairments, also known as the medical listings, which are organized into 14 major body systems for adults and reflect medical conditions that have been determined by the agency to be severe enough to qualify an applicant for benefits. According to SSA officials, there are almost 300 medical impairments organized in 119 listings under the 14 major body systems for adults.

agreement with the Department of Labor's Bureau of Labor Statistics to design, develop, and carry out pilot testing to assess the feasibility of using an existing survey[25] to collect data for an updated system.[26] SSA previously determined that the Department of Labor's existing occupational database, the Occupational Information Network (O*NET), was not sufficiently detailed for evaluating DI and SSI claims, so it would need to develop its own occupational information system. According to SSA officials, the agency still needs to determine exactly how many occupations it will include in its new system, the extent to which it might leverage aspects of O*NET, and the extent to which the new system will include cognitive information. In addition, officials told us that while SSA is currently developing a research plan for fiscal year 2014 and expects that its current approach will cost less and take less time than previously expected, the agency has not yet finalized a cost estimate.

SSA has also taken steps to more fully consider individuals' ability to function with medical impairments in their work or other environments, which is consistent with modern views of disability. For example, SSA has incorporated into some of its medical criteria an assessment of whether a claimant's impairments result in functional limitations that can limit the ability to work and is sponsoring research to more broadly consider how to incorporate these types of assessments in determining disability. However, SSA disagreed with our prior recommendation to conduct limited, focused studies on how to more fully consider factors such as assistive devices and workplace accommodations in its disability determinations,[27] stating that such studies would be inconsistent with Congress' intentions. We noted that Congress has not explicitly prohibited SSA from considering these factors and we believe that conducting these studies would put SSA in a better position to thoughtfully weigh the costs and benefits of these various policy options before deciding on a course of action. After reviewing a draft of our report, the agency said that it would explore the possibility of conducting research in the area of

---

[25]Specifically, the Bureau of Labor Statistics is assessing the feasibility of using the National Compensation Survey.

[26]SSA evaluates claimants' ability to work in the national economy as part of its disability decision-making process. See 42 U.S.C. §§ 423(d), 1382c(a).The occupational information system provides information on jobs in the national economy.

[27]GAO-12-420.

assistive devices but noted that this research would require the involvement of highly specialized medical professionals.

Managing workloads to reduce disability initial claims and hearings backlogs. Although SSA has reported progress with its disability hearings backlog reduction plan, the agency still faces challenges managing significant and persistent disability workload increases, both in terms of initial claims and hearings for appealed claims. SSA has generally increased the number of initial disability claims it has processed annually—completing over 3 million claims each year since fiscal year 2010—but the number of initial claims submitted by applicants has outpaced SSA's effort. Thus, the number of claims awaiting a decision is also growing. SSA's 707,700 initial claims pending in fiscal year 2012 were 27 percent higher than fiscal year 2008 levels. The number of disability beneficiaries is projected to grow about 15 percent between 2012 and 2025. To help manage workloads, Disability Determination Services share work nationally by shifting resources among DDSs on a weekly basis, and dedicated teams in certain states assist by taking claims from states with the highest levels of pending claims. SSA also identifies claimants with the most severe disabilities and expedites decisions on these cases,[28] although they represented less than 6 percent of all initial determinations in September 2012.[29] Most of SSA's regional commissioners told us that simplifying disability policy, such as by streamlining work incentive and work reporting rules, could also help staff better manage disability workloads. Under its regulations, SSA has set forth procedures for testing certain streamlining modifications to its disability determination process.[30] One such modification is the "single

---

[28]SSA has two initiatives to expedite cases for the most severely disabled individuals: Quick Disability Determination and Compassionate Allowances. Using predictive modeling and computer-based screening tools to screen initial applicants, the Quick Disability Determination identifies cases where a favorable disability determination is highly likely and medical evidence is readily available, such as with certain cancers and end-stage renal disease. With Compassionate Allowances, SSA targets the most obviously disabled applicants based on available medical information and generally awards benefits if there is objective medical evidence to confirm the diagnosis and the applicant also meets SSA's non-disability criteria.

[29]SSA derives this percentage by dividing the total number of initial disability claims identified as Quick Disability Determinations, Compassionate Allowances, or both, by the total number of electronic initial disability claims filed in September, the last month of the fiscal year.

[30]20 C.F.R. §§ 404.906, 416.1406.

decisionmaker" approach that allows a disability examiner to make an initial disability determination in most cases without obtaining the signature of a medical or psychological consultant.[31] For example, the examiner can deny an individual whose physical impairments are not expected to meet the duration requirement of 12 months—such as a 26-year-old accident victim who is recovering normally from a recently fractured arm and leg—without the involvement of a medical or psychological consultant. Further, in 10 "prototype" states, in addition to the "single decisionmaker" approach described above, the reconsideration level has been eliminated from the administrative review process.[32] A claimant who is dissatisfied with the initial determination may request a hearing before an administrative law judge. Without reconsiderations, claimants' cases move more quickly to the appeal stage.

With regard to the single decisionmaker approach, many SSA officials told us that it reduces processing time and administrative costs by reserving expensive medical and psychological consultant resources for reviews of more complex cases. With regard to the elimination of reconsiderations, some officials felt that this approach decreases processing time and saves DDS resources, while others feel it contributes to the hearings backlog by adding to the administrative law judges' workloads. Overall, some officials raised concerns that having some states with single decisionmaker authority or no reconsiderations leads to a lack of national uniformity. One association noted that the practice of sharing workloads between states heightens the need for national uniformity. SSA reports that it plans to extend these changes until September 2014, but after that time, the agency will again need to decide whether to extend—and possibly expand—these changes.

While SSA is processing more initial claims annually, claims denied at the initial level can be appealed and often result in a request for a hearing before an administrative law judge. To reduce its hearings backlog, SSA has used strategies such as hiring additional administrative law judges and support staff, opening more hearings offices, and conducting more

---

[31]Medical consultants generally certify all SSI childhood disability claims and all less than fully favorable decisions on DI and SSI claims involving an indication of a mental impairment.

[32]The prototype states also have single decisionmaker authority.

hearings via video conference. Although SSA completed more hearing requests in fiscal year 2012 than in previous years, the agency fell short of its hearings completion target by more than 54,000 hearings and the average wait time for hearings exceeded the agency's target of 321 days by 41 days. SSA officials attribute this missed target and longer wait times for hearings to the increase in claims and delays in the hiring of qualified administrative law judges. At the same time, the agency eliminated most of its oldest pending hearing requests (see fig. 6).

Figure 6: Average Wait Time for SSA Disability Claim Hearings from Request to Decision and Percentage of Offices with Longest Wait Times

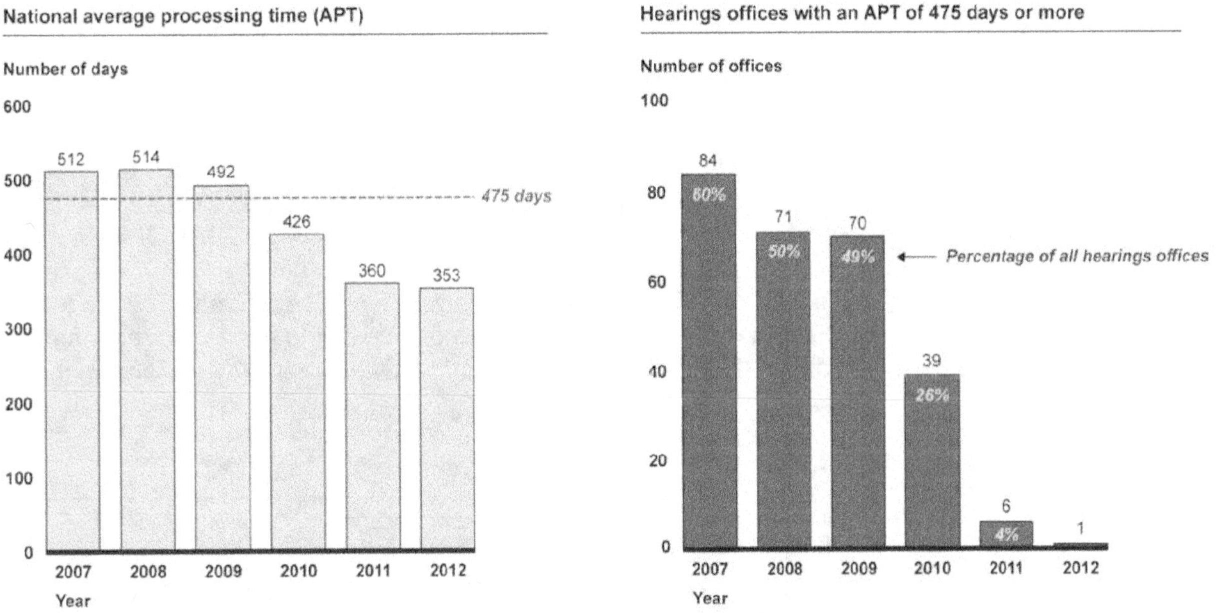

National average processing time (APT)

Number of days

Hearings offices with an APT of 475 days or more

Number of offices

Source: GAO analysis of hearings data from SSA's Case Processing and Management System.

Note: Processing time data refer to the year in which hearing requests were completed.

Ensuring disability program integrity. SSA also faces disability program integrity challenges due to budget decisions and the way it prioritizes competing workload demands such as processing initial claims. Continuing disability reviews (CDR) are periodic reviews that the agency is required to perform to verify that certain recipients still meet SSA disability rules. SSA performs two types of CDRs: medical CDRs to verify that the recipient meets medical criteria and work CDRs to determine if an individual's earnings meet financial criteria. SSA reported that in fiscal year 2010, the agency did not conduct 1.4 million CDRs that were due for review, in part because of competing workloads. In June 2012, we also found that more than 400,000 medical CDRs were overdue for children with mental impairments receiving SSI, with some pending by as many as 13 years or more.[33] Childhood CDRs overall fell from more than 150,000 in fiscal year 2000 to about 45,000 in fiscal year 2011 (a 70 percent decrease). During this time, the number of adult CDRs fell from 584,000 to 179,000.

When CDRs are not conducted as scheduled, some recipients may receive benefits for which they are no longer eligible, and the agency may forgo future program savings. For fiscal year 2010, SSA estimated that every $1 spent on CDRs yielded $9.30 in savings, amounting to a total future savings to federal programs of $3.5 billion.[34] We have previously found that medical and work-related overpayments in the DI program detected by SSA grew from about $860 million in fiscal year 2001 to about $1.4 billion in fiscal year 2010.[35] Despite an increase in DI debt collections—$340 million to $839 million from fiscal year 2001 through fiscal year 2010—outstanding DI debt grew from $2.5 billion to $5.4 billion during this time, including a $225 million increase in fiscal year 2010.[36] Although CDRs are a cost-effective way to help ensure that only those eligible for benefits continue to receive them, SSA officials reported that resource constraints have made it more difficult to remain current on the millions of CDRs it is required to conduct each year, and to balance the

---

[33]GAO, *Supplemental Security Income: Better Management Oversight Needed for Children's Benefits*, GAO-12-497 (Washington, D.C.: June 26, 2012).

[34]This figure represents the present value of future benefits saved for OASDI, SSI, Medicare, and Medicaid. The estimate includes savings to Medicare and Medicaid because in some cases eligibility for SSI and DI confers eligibility for certain Medicare or Medicaid benefits.

[35]GAO, *Disability Insurance: SSA Can Improve Efforts to Detect, Prevent, and Recover Overpayments*, GAO-11-724 (Washington, D.C.: July 27, 2011).

[36]When a DI work-related overpayment is identified, the beneficiary is notified of the overpayment and may request reconsideration or waiver of that overpayment. If SSA denies a reconsideration or waiver request, full repayment is requested. If the beneficiary is receiving DI or certain other SSA benefits, SSA may withhold partial payment of these benefits to recover the debt. However, if no SSA benefits are being received, or if the beneficiary asserts that the proposed withholding amount is too large, the agency generally requests repayment over 12 to 36 months. SSA policy requires a minimum monthly payment of $10. SSA may also attempt to recover payments due from the individual's estate or subsequent survivor's benefits.

competing goals of processing initial claims and reducing its backlogs with ensuring program integrity.

SSA Has Taken Steps to Modernize Its IT Systems to Keep Pace with Workload Demands, but Concerns Remain

IT modernization efforts. SSA has begun to take action on several of our prior recommendations to improve the way it modernizes its IT systems.[37] For example, in May 2012, SSA released its Capital Planning and Investment Control guide. The guide describes the roles and responsibilities of staff under the agency's realigned IT organizational structure[38] and requires that the business case for each of the agency's major IT program include performance measures that will assist the agency in evaluating the program's effectiveness in achieving its goals.[39] SSA also issued an updated IT strategic plan that covers 2012-2016 and supports the updated agency-wide strategic plan.[40] Furthermore, SSA officials told us that they intend to revisit the IT strategic plan annually and refresh it as appropriate. Our prior work indicates that SSA has not always had an updated IT strategic plan to guide its modernization efforts.[41] In the absence of regular updates, SSA based its IT modernization efforts on program activities that were tied to short-term budget cycles and not developed in the context of a long-term strategic plan. While we are encouraged that SSA issued an updated IT strategic plan, at present, it is too soon to assess the extent to which SSA will adhere to the plan and annual reevaluation cycle.

---

[37]GAO, *Social Security Administration: Improved Planning and Performance Measures Are Needed to Help Ensure Successful Technology Modernization,* GAO-12-495. (Washington, D.C.: April 26, 2012).

[38]In 2011, SSA significantly realigned its IT organizational structure—consolidating its Chief Information Officer (CIO) office with its Systems office—but did not conduct an analysis of the realigned functions and how the newly assigned roles and responsibilities would carry out the former Office of CIO functions. Prior to the reorganization, the Office of the CIO's responsibilities included some oversight activities, while the Office of Systems' responsbilities focused more on developing and implementing SSA's systems and enterprise architecture. We previously recommended that SSA define the roles and responsbilities of realigned staff. See GAO-12-495.

[39]We recommended that, for each ongoing modernization initiative, SSA establish performance measures in each of the Office of Management and Budget's (OMB) measurement areas that identify and measure how the investment contributes to meeting goals of the project and of overall modernization efforts.

[40]An in-depth analysis of the plan's technical content was beyond the scope of our review.

[41]GAO-12-495.

SSA is modernizing its IT systems, in part, to support a shift toward offering more online services. As we previously reported, SSA officials have noted that the agency faces several challenges in successfully carrying out IT modernization efforts, including devoting significant resources to the maintenance of existing legacy systems.[42] The agency's expenditures for operations and maintenance increased from $348 million in 2004 to $875 million in 2011.[43] Moreover, SSA's OIG has expressed concerns that the agency is continuing to rely on its legacy applications.[44] For example, many of its programs are written in COBOL,[45] which is one of the oldest computer programming languages and is difficult to modify and update. The OIG noted also that the agency risks losing key institutional knowledge related to COBOL programming and documentation of SSA's increasingly complex information systems. This is of particular concern given the high levels of retirements and attrition the agency has recently experienced and will likely continue to experience. For example, one regional commissioner told us that when an experienced staff person left the region, the remaining staff lacked adequate knowledge of COBOL programming. According to the OIG, SSA has indicated that modernizing its legacy applications will ultimately reduce operating costs and improve service delivery. However, agency officials told us they have conducted analyses that show the costs of moving away from using COBOL currently outweigh the benefits. Accordingly, the OIG found in May 2012 that SSA has developed an approach to gradually reduce its reliance on COBOL for core processing transactions but has not yet articulated a formal strategy for converting its legacy programs to a more modern programming language.[46] SSA officials disagree that such a strategy is needed because they consider this programming language to be sufficient for their needs and point out that it is still used by other businesses.

---

[42]GAO, *Social Security Administration: Technology Modernization Needs Improved Planning and Performance Measures*, GAO-12-723T. (Washington, DC: May 9, 2012).

[43]GAO-12-495.

[44]SSA OIG, *The Social Security Administration's Software Modernization and Use of Common Business Oriented Language*, A-14-11-11132. (Baltimore, MD: May 17, 2012).

[45]SSA relies on legacy applications programmed with Common Business Oriented Language, or COBOL. COBOL was introduced in 1959 and became the first widely used, high-level programming language for business applications.

[46]SSA OIG, A-14-11-11132.

Information security weaknesses. In recent years, SSA has been challenged to effectively protect its computer systems and networks, particularly with regard to internal security weaknesses. SSA uses and stores a great deal of sensitive information, including financial and medical information and Social Security numbers. Our prior work states that it is essential for agencies to have information security controls that ensure sensitive information is adequately protected from inadvertent or deliberate misuse, fraudulent use, and improper disclosure, modification, or destruction.[47] However, in fiscal year 2012, SSA's OIG identified weaknesses in some of the agency's information security program components that limited SSA's overall effectiveness in protecting the agency's information and information systems.[48] For example, auditors were able to gain access to Social Security numbers and other sensitive information through an SSA intranet search engine. According to the OIG, these weaknesses constituted a significant deficiency in the agency's information security program under the Federal Information Security Management Act of 2002 (FISMA).[49] In addition, in its fiscal year 2012 report on SSA's major management challenges, the OIG stated that weaknesses in certain elements of the agency's information security program may challenge the agency's ability to use its IT infrastructure to support current and future workloads. Furthermore, in the same year, the agency's independent financial auditor also identified a material weakness in information systems controls over financial management

---

[47]GAO, *Transportation: Key Issues and Management Challenges*, GAO-12-581T. (Washington, D.C., March 29, 2012).

[48]These weaknesses were identified in the areas of continuous monitoring, configuration management, identity and access management, risk management, and contractor systems oversight. See SSA OIG, *The Social Security Administration's Compliance with the Federal Information Security Management Act of 2002 for Fiscal Year 2012*, A-14-12-12120. (Baltimore, MD: November 15, 2012).

[49]FISMA was enacted as title III of the E-Government Act of 2002, Pub. L. No. 107-347, 116 Stat. 2899, 2946. According to OMB, a significant deficiency is a weakness in an agency's overall information systems security program or management control structure, or within one or more information systems, that significantly restricts the capability of the agency to carry out its mission or compromises the security of its information, information systems, personnel, or other resources, operations, or assets. In this context, the risk is great enough that the agency head and outside agencies must be notified and immediate or near-immediate corrective action must be taken. See OMB, "Memorandum for Heads of Executive Departments and Agencies: FY 2012 Reporting Instructions for the Federal Information Security Management Act and Agency Privacy Management," (September 27, 2012).

GAO-13-459 SSA Management Challenges

statements based on several concerns, many of which have been longstanding (see fig. 7).[50]

Figure 7: Weaknesses Identified in SSA's Information Security Program, Fiscal Years 2009–2012

	2009	2010	2011	2012
Entity wide security program				
Lack of monitoring and policy implementation related to the configuration and information content of SSA's Intranet Webpages	☐	☐	☐	■
Lack of controls related to identifying and monitoring high-risk programs operating on the agency's mainframe	☐	■	■	■
Insufficient vulnerability testing conducted by the agency to identify critical weaknesses in its IT environment	☐	☐	■	■
Access controls				
Lack of a comprehensive user profile and access recertification program	■	■	■	■
Lack of appropriate controls to prevent unauthorized access to the agency's production environment for Benefit Payment Applications	☐	☐	☐	■
Compensating controls				
Weaknesses over approving and documenting changes to SSA software applications	☐	■	■	■
Weaknesses over physical access controls	☐	■	■	■
Weaknesses over ensuring that system users have appropriate access to various system resouces	☐	■	■	■

Source: GAO analysis of SSA's Financial Statement Audit Reports, fiscal years 2009-2012.

SSA is implementing a multi-year plan of corrective actions to address many of these weaknesses. For example, while SSA is currently reviewing access rights for different types of system users[51] to identify any cases where employees have inappropriate access to sensitive information, officials told us the process is very time-consuming and the agency does not expect to complete its review of the highest-risk profiles until 2014.[52] In addition to reviewing access rights, SSA officials told us the agency purchased software in 2011 that monitors the agency's information systems to detect potential data breach incidents. Agency

---

[50]In this context, the external auditors, Grant Thornton, LLP, defined a material weakness as one or more deficiencies in internal controls such that there is a reasonable possibility that a material misstatement of the entity's financial statements will not be prevented or detected and corrected on a timely basis. A deficiency in internal control exists when the design or operation of a control does not allow management or employees, in the normal course of performing their assigned functions, to prevent, or detect and correct misstatements on a timely basis.

[51]SSA employees are granted access to different aspects of SSA's system depending on the nature of the work they do.

[52]There are 702 profiles which are considered to be the highest-risk. The highest-risk profiles are those for users of applications that support the agency's financial management systems.

officials told us they are currently in the process of implementing and fine-tuning the software.

However, the OIG raised concerns about how the agency has previously prioritized information security within its larger IT budget. Specifically, it stated that one of the underlying causes for these weaknesses is that SSA needed to strategically allocate sufficient resources to resolve or prevent high-risk security weaknesses in a more timely fashion.[53] For example, SSA officials told us that, in some cases, security employees' time is primarily spent performing duties that do not address the IT security weaknesses identified by external financial auditors and OIG.[54] Though SSA officials emphasized that the information security risks identified were internal,[55] inappropriate internal access to or misuse of sensitive information can have a significant impact. For example, according to the OIG, in 2012, a former SSA employee was found to have used her position to provide personally identifiable information to a person outside the agency, who is accused of using the information for criminal purposes.

SSA Is Taking Steps to Centralize Facilities Management but Lacks a Proactive Approach to Evaluate Its Office Space

Centralizing facilities management. SSA is beginning to centralize its facilities management, but officials indicated it may lead to a trade-off between efficiency and flexibility. The agency administers its programs and services through a network of over 1,700 facilities, consisting of government-owned and leased buildings, which costs approximately $700 million annually, according to SSA.[56] As shown in Figure 8, these facilities fall into three categories: headquarters facilities located predominantly in the Baltimore/Washington, D.C. metropolitan area, an extensive network of field-based facilities used to process initial claims and post-entitlement

---

[53]SSA OIG, A-14-12-12120.

[54]Such tasks include establishing a formalized process to test transactions associated with access profiles.

[55]The OIG and external auditors did not perform external penetration tests during their audits.

[56]SSA leases all of its space, approximately 30 million square feet as of the end of fiscal year 2012, from the General Services Administration (GSA). Approximately one-third of that space is in government-owned buildings and the remaining two-thirds in government-leased buildings.

actions,[57] and a network of facilities that carry out the agency's disability adjudication and review process. The agency has had a more decentralized facilities management process, but officials told us they are currently moving all facilities management under SSA's Office of Facilities and Supply Management (OFSM). Some officials have told us that this centralization can lead to greater efficiencies and standardization, but cautioned that there may be a trade-off in terms of flexibility and awareness of local circumstances at the regional level. For example, some regional commissioners told us that facilities decisions made at the headquarters level may not take into account the layout of specific buildings or how construction seasons vary in different locations.

Figure 8: Number of SSA Facilities by Component and Type (as of Fiscal Year 2012)

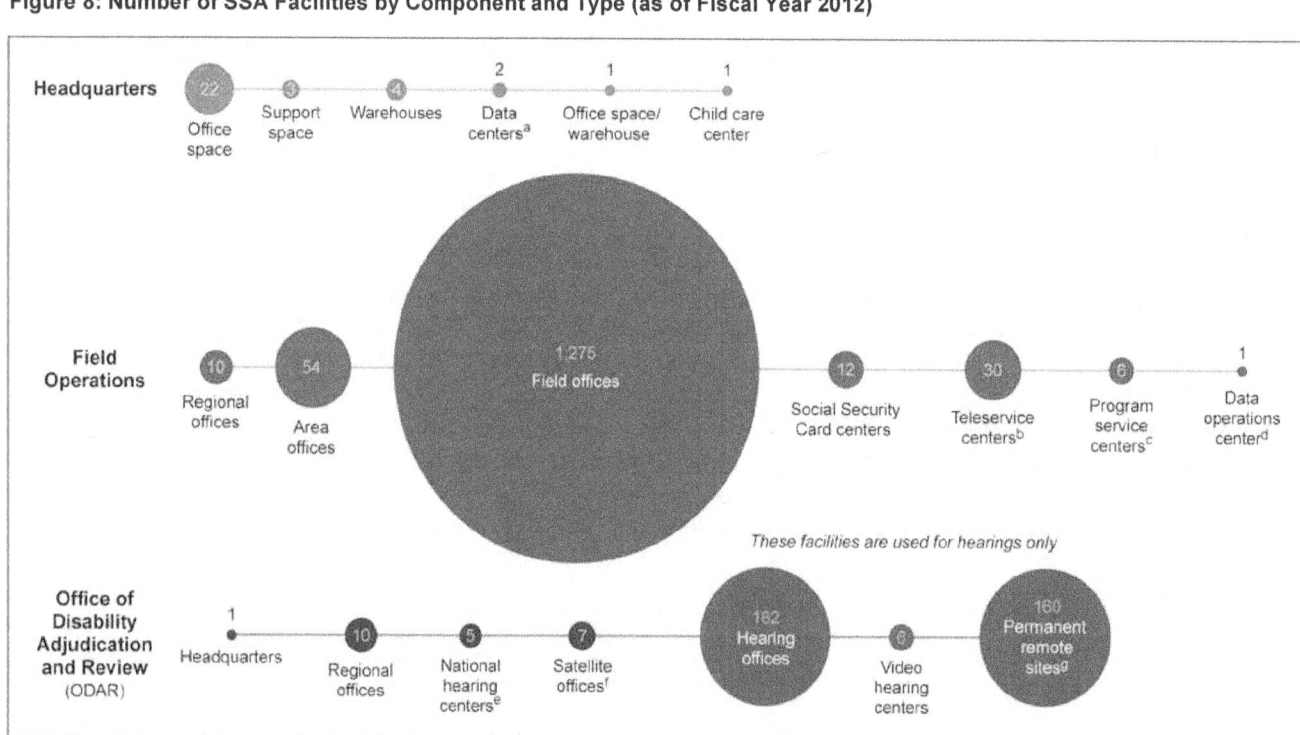

Source: GAO analysis of SSA data from its Office of Facilities and Supply Management.

[57]Post-entitlement actions include such things as address changes and updating beneficiary earnings.

[a]SSA's data center, the National Computer Center, and its backup, the Second Support Center, store data and house the backbone of the agency's automated systems. SSA is currently constructing a new data center to replace the National Computer Center, which was built in 1979.

[b]Teleservice centers handle general inquiries from the public, simple post-entitlement actions, and referrals from field offices.

[c]Program service centers handle complex claims and post-entitlement actions.

[d]Among other responsibilities, the data operations center handles various customer service workloads, including providing technical and benefit information on SSA programs by phone.

[e]National hearing centers handle workloads from backlogged hearing offices.

[f]Satellite offices provide support to their parent hearing offices.

[g]At permanent remote sites, hearings are held in person with a traveling administrative law judge or by video. Of the 160 permanent remote sites, SSA told us that 148 are located within SSA field offices.

Limited facilities planning efforts. A contractor hired by the General Services Administration is currently working on a long-term plan for SSA's headquarters facilities, the Master Housing Plan.[58] An SSA official told us that the contractor has solicited input and feedback from the agency on the draft plan. According to the National Research Council, a free exchange of information among the various stakeholders can make decision-making for facilities investments more accurate and effective.[59] However, an SSA official told us the agency lacks a comprehensive planning effort that encompasses all of the agency's facilities.

Efforts to reduce office space. SSA officials told us the agency is engaged in ongoing efforts to reduce the footprint of its headquarters facilities. According to a senior SSA official, vacant space in headquarters facilities has increased during the past few years as a result of the shrinking workforce.[60] Using the agency's Large Site Space Standards,[61]

---

[58]Earlier drafts of the Master Housing Plan were developed by GSA and OFSM. For the current stage, GSA engaged a contractor to carry out the study, according to SSA officials.

[59]The National Research Council is part of the National Academy of Sciences. See National Research Council. *Investments in Federal Facilities: Asset Management Strategies for the 21st Century.* (Washington, D.C.: 2004).

[60]This official estimated that, as of February 28, 2013, there were approximately 800-1,000 vacant workspaces in SSA headquarters facilities.

[61]SSA's Large Site Space Standards lay out the criteria for allocating space according to staffing levels and other factors.

SSA officials told us that OFSM is analyzing the space needs of all offices in the headquarters area and will reassign space according to these criteria. A senior official told us that SSA's efforts were motivated by several factors, including an OMB directive to make more efficient use of federal office space;[62] the agency's ultimate goal of terminating commercial leasing for most office space in the headquarters area; and, to a lesser degree, reducing current vacancies in headquarters.

In addition to these headquarters-focused efforts, SSA is reducing office space in the field as opportunities arise, but it lacks a proactive plan to assess field facilities for potential space reductions. When OFSM reviews a field-based space action (e.g., lease renewal, move, renovation), an SSA official told us that the proposed action is assessed to identify if there are opportunities to reduce or otherwise change the facility's space allocation. For example, after such an assessment, the Denver regional office space was reduced by one-third. However, OFSM's standards do not call for wholesale reductions or reconfigurations of existing space. SSA has established a workgroup that is developing guidance to help identify opportunities to reduce space by co-locating certain field-based facilities, such as field offices and video-based disability hearing offices. Officials told us that in January 2013, they endorsed the workgroup's final recommendations and proposals as the formal agency policy.

Considerations for realigning the facilities structure. SSA has been advised to consider aligning its facilities structure with its changing methods of providing services. For example, SSA's OIG reported in 2011 that SSA's long-term planning efforts should assess whether the number, size, geographic coverage, and staffing of the agency's existing office structure are in line with future methods of providing customer service.[63] In 2011, the Social Security Advisory Board suggested that as SSA continues to increase electronic service delivery, the agency should adapt its organizational structure to maximize the effectiveness of the agency's transformation. At the same time, SSA has long considered face-to-face

---

[62]In May 2012, OMB's Acting Director released a memo, which calls for agencies to make more efficient use of the government's real estate assets and generally prohibits agencies from increasing their real estate inventory, or footprint. See OMB, "Memorandum to the Heads of Executive Agencies and Departments: Promoting Efficient Spending to Support Agency Operations," (May 11, 2012).

[63]SSA OIG, *The Social Security Administration's Customer Service Delivery Plan*, A-07-11-01125. (Baltimore, MD: July 2011).

GAO-13-459 SSA Management Challenges

interaction to be the gold standard of customer service, and an official has told us that any changes away from that model would represent a major cultural shift for the agency.

In prior work, we have reported that federal agencies may be able to increase efficiency and effectiveness by consolidating physical infrastructure or management functions, and several agencies have already undertaken consolidation efforts.[64] For example, in 2000, the Internal Revenue Service began consolidating its individual paper processing centers to reduce overhead and real estate costs and improve efficiency in response to increases in electronic filing; the agency estimates that the initiative saved $175 million through 2011. Over the past 6 years, the U.S. Postal Service has taken several actions to reduce the footprint of its retail space, including two nationwide initiatives to review its facilities for possible closure. The Census Bureau announced plans in 2011 to close 6 of its 12 regional offices by 2013 to reduce the cost and improve the quality of surveys the Census Bureau conducts annually; the Census Bureau estimates the initiative will save $15-18 million annually beginning in fiscal year 2014. SSA officials told us they have spoken with GSA officials about consolidation, but have not consulted with any of these agencies to learn about their experiences in considering and implementing significant changes to their facilities structures.

SSA has begun to take advantage of opportunities to consolidate or co-locate offices in the regions. SSA regional commissioners told us that field offices have been consolidated in most of its 10 regions.[65] Regional commissioners told us that consolidations reduce such expenses as rent and guard services, and a single office consolidation can save as much as $2-3 million dollars over a 10-year period. Furthermore, regional commissioners told us that several regions have co-located with the Office of Disability Adjudication and Review to provide space to hold

---

[64]GAO, *Streamlining Government: Questions to Consider When Evaluating Proposals to Consolidate Physical Infrastructure and Management Functions*, GAO-12-542. (Washington, D.C.: May 23, 2012).

[65]SSA officials told us that offices are consolidated by closing an office and moving its staff into another office. Consolidations often occur by merging two offices that are located very close together, or when staffing in one office has fallen below levels needed to sustain the office. In cases where offices are closed because of prohibitively low staffing levels, the remaining staff are generally absorbed into nearby offices.

GAO-13-459 SSA Management Challenges

hearings within field offices. A regional commissioner told us that when these co-located offices share space, such as waiting areas, SSA saves money on guard services and rent.

Despite these actions, an SSA official told us that the agency has not engaged in a systematic analysis of potential approaches for consolidating its facilities or realigning its facilities with the agency's evolving service delivery model. The National Research Council recommends that federal agencies use their organizational mission to guide facilities investment decisions and then integrate these investments into their strategic planning processes. We previously reported that agencies should consider the potential costs and benefits of consolidation over the long term.[66] For example, consolidation is not beneficial in all instances, such as in rural areas where people would have to travel a considerable distance to reach the nearest office. Therefore, it is important to evaluate the goals of the consolidation against the realistic possibility of the extent to which those goals would be achieved. Furthermore, our previous work suggests that consolidation initiatives can be immensely complex, politically charged, and costly; even decisions to consolidate individual offices can create challenges. For example, a regional commissioner told us that a recent proposal to save money by consolidating two nearby offices in a major urban area was met with substantial resistance from the community and elected officials. Our prior work states that decision makers need to balance the benefits of consolidation against the physical, up-front financial, bureaucratic, and political costs, while considering alternatives. To assess the potential impact and challenges of consolidation, we suggested that agencies consider likely costs and benefits of the consolidation, how to fund up-front costs associated with consolidation, and the effect on various stakeholders. (See app. II for a list of key questions that can be used to assess potential consolidation initiatives.)

---

[66]GAO-12-542.

SSA's Planning Efforts Are Not Adequate to Address the Long-Term Nature of Its Management Challenges

SSA has ongoing planning efforts, but we have identified two major areas in which these efforts have fallen short in addressing the long-term nature of the agency's management challenges: (1) its planning efforts are short-term and do not adequately address emerging issues, and (2) it lacks continuity in its strategic planning leadership. As the prior section discussed, over the next decade, the agency's workloads will increase while its workforce will likely decrease, raising questions about how SSA can best deploy its human capital and information technology resources and best align its disability policy and physical infrastructure to meet these demands. Practices such as involving stakeholders and planning for different scenarios are considered key for successful long-term planning efforts, which SSA's current planning efforts do not include.

Need for longer-term efforts to address emerging issues. SSA's planning efforts, from an overall strategic plan to its service delivery plan, typically look no more than 5 years out. For example, SSA is finalizing a service delivery plan, but the draft document primarily contains detailed plans for the next 5 years and focuses on existing initiatives rather than articulating specific long-term strategies for the agency's service delivery model. The plan was developed as a companion to the agency's strategic plan,[67] which defines the agency's goals for the next 4 years.[68] While the draft service delivery plan acknowledges the need to assess the agency's workforce structure, it stops short of providing a vision for how the workforce structure should best make use of expanded virtual and automated service delivery channels. The draft raises the possibility of developing a more generalized workforce by training employees to handle a variety of different workloads or centralizing the most complex workloads by assigning them to technical staff specifically trained to handle them, but it does not advocate for either of these approaches or provide a detailed analysis of their relative merits. Similarly, the plan states that the following issues will need to be considered over the next 6 to 10 years, but it does not provide a specific strategy for how to resolve the need to:

---

[67]SSA addresses core IT updates separately in a 5-year IT strategic plan.

[68]OMB guidance directs agencies to have strategic plans covering a period of no less than 4 years. Agencies may set strategic plan goals for longer periods of time.

- strategically develop and place self-service options, such as electronic kiosks;

- determine whether the Internet should be the primary service delivery mechanism for certain services; and

- standardize fees SSA already charges and determine whether it is appropriate for the agency to charge fees for additional services.[69]

Further, the plan does not articulate SSA's long-term costs and benefits for its investments, such as the specific impact that moving to online services is expected to have on backlogs and workforce needs. For many years, we have recommended that SSA develop a comprehensive service delivery plan that outlines how it will deliver quality service while managing growing work demands within a constrained budget.[70]

Similarly, SSA's current strategic plan largely describes the continuation, expansion, or enhancement of existing activities, rather than proposing new initiatives or broad changes to address emerging issues. One of the goals of the agency's strategic plan is to increase the public's use of online services, but several SSA officials and representatives of one SSA management group told us that this shift will not be sufficient to address growing service demands. For example, as discussed earlier, to meet service challenges, some officials said the agency will also need to simplify its disability policy. They also told us the agency will need to develop a strategy for meeting the needs of vulnerable populations who may not have access to computers at home or who may not be computer literate. At the same time, however, some SSA officials noted that the agency may need to limit the number of days per week that field offices are open to the public to contain costs.

---

[69]Examples of services for which SSA may charge a standard fee include copying folders, forwarding letters, manually performing a Social Security number verification for a third party, and responding to requests for a W-2 or W-3 for Social Security benefits received.

[70]See GAO, *Social Security Administration: Service Delivery Plan Needed to Address Baby Boom Retirement Challenges*, GAO-09-24 (Washington, D.C.: Jan. 9, 2009); *Social Security: Sustained Effort Needed to Improve Management and Prepare for the Future*, GAO/HRD-94-22 (Washington, D.C.: Oct. 27, 1993); *SSA's Management Challenges: Strong Leadership Needed to Turn Plans Into Timely Meaningful Action*, GAO/T-HEHS-98-113 (Washington, D.C.: Mar. 12, 1998); and *Social Security Administration: Effective Leadership Needed to Meet Daunting Challenges*, GAO/HEHS-96-196 (Washington, D.C.: Sept.12, 1996).

Various groups have called on SSA to acknowledge emerging long-term issues by articulating them in a longer-term strategy. In 2011, the Social Security Advisory Board called for SSA to develop a strategy for service delivery through 2020 that will serve as the cornerstone for its IT, human capital, policy review, and organizational restructuring plans.[71] The SSA OIG also called on SSA to prepare a longer-term vision to ensure that it has the programs, processes, staff, and infrastructure necessary to provide service in the future.[72] Regional commissioners and field managers said that a long-term service delivery plan could help to clarify issues such as what services will be available online in the future, how these services will be implemented, how IT modernization will support service delivery, which offices will have responsibility for different workloads, how the agency will use telework, and how the agency will approach workload sharing. In addition, GAO's internal controls guidance states that federal agencies should comprehensively identify risks, analyze and decide how to manage these risks, and establish mechanisms to deal with continual changes in governmental, economic, industry, regulatory, and operating conditions.[73] SSA prepared its last long-term agency vision—which covered a 10-year period—in 2000, motivated by many conditions which remain true today, such as increasing workloads, advances in technology, and employee retirements. A former SSA official knowledgeable about the development of the *2010 Vision* told us that unlike the agency's strategic plan, which addressed incremental changes, the long-term vision addressed broader issues and allowed the agency to consider more transformative changes.

Senior agency officials told us that as an agency, SSA generally views long-term planning as a secondary responsibility and is more focused on addressing short-term, tactical issues. As one official said, agency officials are addressing immediate concerns and not thinking, for example, about what the agency's field operations should look like in 10 years. Several officials also noted that uncertainty about budget resources has made it difficult for SSA to engage in multi-year planning.

---

[71]Social Security Advisory Board. *A Vision of the Future for the Social Security Administration,* (Washington, D.C.: March 2011).

[72]SSA OIG. *Fiscal Year 2012 Inspector General Statement on the Social Security Administration's Major Management and Performance Challenges,* A-02-13-13041 (Nov. 8, 2012).

[73]GAO/AIMD-00-21.3.1.

One official commented that as a result of its budget situation, the agency has been reactive and failed to consider big picture issues.

Need for continuity in strategic planning leadership. Senior officials said that SSA should dedicate a position, such as a chief strategic officer, that will report directly to the Commissioner and be solely responsible for strategic planning in order to bring sustained, focused attention to long-term management challenges. The GPRA Modernization Act of 2010 charges top agency leadership with improving agency management and performance.[74] Agency leaders are responsible for setting near-term and long-term goals; conducting data-driven progress reviews; and assuring that decision-makers at all levels of the organization have timely, actionable performance information. SSA previously had an Office of the Chief Strategic Officer, which was responsible for overseeing strategic planning. This office worked with all SSA components to prioritize initiatives that would help the agency meet its goals and determined how to link these initiatives to the agency's budget. However, the office was dissolved in May 2008 and since that time, the agency has not had an office dedicated to strategic planning. Deputy commissioners with temporary responsibility for strategic planning have led the efforts to develop SSA's last two strategic plans. One senior official told us that efforts to develop component-level plans, such as the strategic human capital plan and IT strategic plan, have not been well coordinated with the development of the agency-wide strategic plan. Another senior official said that a chief strategic officer could think about the agency in totality, building connections across organizational silos, in part because this individual would not have a stake in a particular component. For example, such a leader could consider interconnections between the agency's IT capabilities and its human capital structure when planning for the future.

Key long-term planning practices that could be employed. Strategic planning literature and experts cite the following as key long-term planning practices that could be employed by SSA to successfully address these issues:

- **Begin early in a new leader's tenure.** Several SSA officials we spoke with told us that developing a long-term service delivery plan should be the next commissioner's top priority. One former senior

---

[74]Pub. L. No. 111-352, § 8, 124 Stat. 3866, 3878 (2011).

SSA official familiar with the development of *2010 Vision* told us that the document was developed during a former commissioner's final year in office. Consequently, it was not embraced by the next leadership team, who wanted to create their own vision. This official recommended that the next commissioner develop a long-term vision early in his or her term.

- **Involve stakeholders from across the agency to obtain buy-in.** The long-term plan should be developed with input from key stakeholders and constituents, such as employee unions, who will be affected by the plan, and the organization should ensure that communication is open and two-way throughout the process. Otherwise, these groups could resist the plan's implementation.

- **Develop performance goals and measures.** The long-term vision should be linked to short-term goals and a system for accountability. Performance measures also allow officials to consider the relative merits of alternative strategies if the stated objective is not met.

- **Leadership should support the plan.** The long-term plan needs backing from top agency management. Leadership support is demonstrated by allocating appropriate resources. For example, the office leading the planning effort should have sufficient standing within the organization, as well as staff dedicated to the effort on a day-to-day basis.

- **Prepare for different scenarios.** Several officials raised concerns that variability in the agency's budget and IT developments make it difficult to plan for the future. However, strategic planning literature touts the success of organizations that are flexible and adaptive. These organizations consider plausible future alternatives and use them to generate strategic options.

- **Align interim plans to the long-term strategy.** Concepts in the long-term plan should drive the agency's other plans (e.g., human capital, information technology, facilities).

Conclusions

The challenges SSA faces will substantially affect its ability to address critical concerns in the coming years. SSA's efforts to meet many of its management challenges have been complicated by budgetary constraints and continued uncertainty about the current and future fiscal environment. Despite these constraints, the agency will need to balance competing demands for resources—both in terms of managing day-to-day budget decisions and planning for emerging and long-term budget issues. SSA already manages a substantial and diverse workload and the demands on SSA from new retirees and individuals with disabilities will continue to grow. Without prompt action to address these challenges, the agency jeopardizes its ability to provide quality service to the public while meeting other critical responsibilities such as ensuring program integrity and administering any changes made to protect the solvency of the Social Security trust funds. In particular, if the agency does not develop specific strategies to address attrition, including ongoing retirements, it risks losing institutional knowledge and expertise at a time when workloads and service demands are increasing. Moreover, while SSA has increased the proportion of its services that it delivers electronically, it has not conducted an analysis to determine whether realigning its existing and future headquarters, region, and field office structure could more effectively and efficiently support the agency's mission.

SSA's new commissioner will face wide-ranging challenges that will require a comprehensive, long-range strategy that current planning efforts do not adequately address. The interrelated nature of SSA's challenges reinforces the need for a long-term and integrated strategy to help ensure that future actions are coordinated and efficient. Also, without a dedicated entity to provide sustained leadership, SSA's planning efforts will likely remain decentralized and short-term. In the absence of a long-term strategy for service delivery, the agency will be poorly positioned to make needed well-informed decisions about its critical functions, including how many and what type of employees SSA will need for its future workforce, how the agency will address disability claims backlogs while ensuring program integrity, and how the agency will more strategically use its information technology and physical infrastructure to best deliver services. Given its budget constraints, SSA needs a solid, long-term strategy to guide decisions about how to best leverage its limited resources.

Recommendations for Executive Action

We recommend that the incoming Commissioner of Social Security:

1. Elevate the agency's strategic planning efforts by considering having an entity or individual dedicated to ensuring that these activities are coordinated agency-wide.

2. Prepare for wide-ranging management challenges by developing a long-term strategy for service delivery.

3. Mitigate the potential loss of institutional knowledge and expertise and help ensure leadership continuity by directing the Deputy Commissioner of Human Resources to update the agency's succession plan.

4. Determine if realigning the agency's headquarters, regional, or field office structure could yield increases in the agency's effectiveness and efficiency by launching an exploratory effort to assess the utility and feasibility of such a realignment or consolidation. These efforts could include holding discussions with other federal agencies, such as the Census Bureau and the Internal Revenue Service, to learn about their experiences undergoing similar transformations and studying the likely costs and benefits of consolidation, as well as other potential impacts.

Agency Comments

We provided a draft of this report to SSA for review and comment. In its written comments, reproduced in appendix III, SSA agreed with our 4 recommendations. In responding to a copy of our draft report, SSA noted that the agency recently appointed a Chief Strategic Officer who reports directly to the Commissioner and will be responsible for coordinating agency-wide strategic planning efforts. SSA told us that this official will also lead an agency-wide effort to develop a long-range strategic plan that will integrate information technology, service delivery, and human capital plans. They told us they will seek input from various stakeholders, including employees, advocates, and Congress, and expect to complete the long-range plan by February 2015 and to release it with the President's Budget for fiscal year 2016. In addition, SSA told us that they re-implemented their national Leadership Development Program in spring 2013 and plan to update their succession plan in calendar year 2013. Finally, the agency has agreed to begin exploring its field, regional, and headquarters organizational structures to find ways to increase efficiency and effectiveness and to initiate discussions with other federal agencies to learn about their experiences with similar efforts. SSA also provided technical comments that we have incorporated, as appropriate.

We are sending copies of this report to the Commissioner of Social Security, appropriate congressional committees, and other interested parties. In addition, the report is available at no charge on the GAO website at http://www.gao.gov.

If you or your staff have any questions about this report, please contact me at (202) 512-7215 or bertonid@gao.gov. Contact points for our Offices of Congressional Relations and Public Affairs may be found on the last page of this report. GAO staff who made major contributions to this report are listed in appendix IV.

Sincerely yours,

Daniel Bertoni
Director
Education, Workforce,
   and Income Security Issues

Appendix I: Objectives, Scope, and Methodology

The objectives of this review focused on (1) key management challenges SSA faces in meeting its mission-related objectives and (2) the extent to which SSA's planning efforts address these challenges.

To identify SSA's key management challenges, we conducted in-depth interviews with the SSA Office of the Inspector General (OIG) and the Social Security Advisory Board. We also reviewed SSA OIG's "Statement on SSA's Major Management and Performance Challenges" reports from fiscal years 2001-2012. In addition, we reviewed relevant reports from GAO, SSA OIG, and the Social Security Advisory Board. We also reviewed the SSA's agency-wide strategic plan.

To learn about SSA's key management challenges and the extent to which SSA's planning efforts address these challenges, we conducted in-depth interviews with SSA officials from headquarters and in the field. At SSA headquarters, we interviewed officials from the Office of the Chief Actuary; the Office of Budget, Finance, and Management; the Office of Disability Adjudication and Review; the Office of Human Resources; the Office of Operations; the Office of Quality Performance; the Office of Retirement and Disability Policy; the Office of Systems; and the Office of the Commissioner. We also conducted semi-structured interviews with SSA's regional commissioners and officials from groups that represent state and federal SSA employees, including the National Council of Social Security Administration Field Operations Locals (American Federation of Government Employees), the National Council of Social Security Management Associations, the National Council of Disability Determination Directors, and the National Association of Disability Examiners. During these semi-structured interviews, we asked each interviewee the same series of questions addressing each of the agency's major long-term management challenges (human capital, disability programs, information technology, and physical infrastructure) and service delivery. We also reviewed applicable federal laws and regulations.

To learn about the extent to which SSA's planning efforts address management challenges, we reviewed key agency planning and other documents, such as SSA's current strategic plan, strategic human capital plan, most recent Retirement Wave report, strategic leadership succession plan, IT strategic plan, IT capital investment process guide, facilities standards, and the agency-wide draft service delivery plan. We also reviewed GAO's internal control standards; Executive Order 13,327, entitled "Federal Real Property Asset Management;" the GPRA

Modernization Act of 2010; and relevant GAO, SSA OIG, and Social
Security Advisory Board reports.

To better understand the key management challenges facing the agency,
we obtained SSA data from a number of administrative and management
information systems. We obtained background data about the actual and
projected number of benefit outlays, beneficiaries, and claimants from the
Office of the Chief Actuary. We also obtained data about actual and
projected retirements and retirement eligibility of headquarters and field
managers, supervisors, and staff from SSA's Human Resources
Operational Data Store. To learn about the agency's disability claims
backlog and hearings wait time, we obtained agency data from the
agency's fiscal year 2012 Performance and Accountability Report and
Case Processing and Management System. We also obtained data about
the SSA's administrative expenditures for its major benefit programs from
the Office of Budget. In addition, we obtained data on SSA's facilities by
type from the Office of Facilities and Supply Management. To learn about
SSA employee morale, we also obtained data from the Office of
Personnel Management's Federal Employee Viewpoint Survey. We
assessed the reliability of these data by reviewing related documentation
and interviewing knowledgeable agency officials, and we determined
these data were sufficiently reliable for our needs.

To identify key long-term planning practices, we conducted a literature
search. We sought documents that describe the benefits of long-term
planning, the elements of a long-term vision, and the process for
developing such a plan. To identify relevant literature, we searched
bibliographic databases covering scholarly and peer-reviewed material;
trade and industry articles; and publications from associations and
nonprofit and think tank organizations, such as ProQuest, WorldCat,
ECO/ArticleFirst/PapersFirst, and Dialog. We restricted our search to
U.S.-based materials published between 2002 and 2012. The search
identified over 900 articles, of which 28 were deemed to be relevant to
our work. We also consulted with long-term planning experts.

We conducted this performance audit from September 2012 to May 2013
in accordance with generally accepted government auditing standards.
Those standards require that we plan and perform the audit to obtain
sufficient, appropriate evidence to provide a reasonable basis for our
findings and conclusions based on our audit objectives. We believe that
the evidence obtained provides a reasonable basis for our findings and
conclusions based on our audit objectives.

Appendix II: Key Questions to Consider When Evaluating Consolidation Proposals

In 2012, we reported a list of key questions for federal agencies to consider when evaluating proposals to consolidate physical infrastructure and management functions.[1] The key questions and additional sub-questions listed below address the ideas, strategies, and leading practices that may facilitate consolidations. However, the list is not exhaustive, nor is it necessary for an agency to consider every listed question.

What are the goals of the consolidation? What opportunities will be addressed through the consolidation and what problems will be solved? What problems, if any, will be created?

- Have agency leaders identified specific goals to be achieved through consolidation?

- Have agency leaders assessed how consolidation can help an agency incorporate changes in technology, business processes, or the needs of customers or clients?

- How have agency leaders weighed the importance of achieving the goals against a realistic assessment of the effort that will be required to achieve them?

- How have agency leaders considered the risks to consolidation that could prevent the achievement of goals and planned for ways to manage them?

- Are agency leaders defining the benefits associated with consolidation and describing how the future will be both different from and better than the past?

- Are agency leaders providing a clear and compelling picture of what will constitute success?

---

[1]See GAO, *Streamlining Government: Questions to Consider When Evaluating Proposals to Consolidate Physical Infrastructure and Management Functions*, GAO-12-542. (Washington, D.C.: May 23, 2012). These questions were identified based on GAO's extensive body of work on government reform, a literature review on public sector consolidations, and interviews with practitioners and academic experts in public management and government reform.

What will be the likely costs and benefits of the consolidation? Are sufficiently reliable data available to support a business-case analysis or cost-benefit analysis?

- What data on the likely costs and benefits of a consolidation are available?

- Are the data sufficiently accurate and reliable? What data on the likely costs and benefits of a consolidation are unavailable, and has a plan been developed to mitigate the unavailability or unreliability of certain data?

- On the basis of the data available, can a reasonable expectation of a consolidation's costs and benefits be drawn?

- Have the likely costs and benefits been subjected to a sensitivity analysis? How sensitive are the estimated costs and benefits to variation in less reliable data or other key assumptions?

How can the up-front costs associated with the consolidation be funded?

- Can immediate efficiencies or uncommitted funds in other areas be redirected to pay for the up-front costs of a consolidation?

- Has the agency considered how it will assess return on investment for any funding for up-front costs?

- Can a working capital fund or other funds be drawn on as a funding mechanism?

- Is Congress amenable to establishing a funding mechanism for a consolidation and appropriating funds for it?

Who are the consolidation stakeholders, and how will they be affected? How have the stakeholders been involved in the decision, and how have their views been considered? On balance, do stakeholders understand the rationale for consolidation?

- Have agency leaders identified affected stakeholders?

- Have agency leaders determined the necessary frequency and timing of communication about the consolidation to internal and external stakeholders?

- Does the communication strategy allow for a two-way exchange of information between management and stakeholders?

- How is the agency planning to involve employees to obtain their ideas and get their support? Have union representatives been consulted? Are there employee task teams responsible for developing and proposing common solutions to particular issues related to the consolidation?

- How does the agency plan to provide information to employees about how their jobs might be affected, what their rights and protections might be, or how their responsibilities might change with the new organization?

- Is the agency planning to communicate information through different channels such as e-mail, face-to-face meetings, large and small group meetings, intranet websites, and town hall meetings?

To what extent do plans show that change management practices[2] will be used to implement the consolidation?

Will top leadership be engaged in driving the consolidation plan?

- Do agency leaders have plans to move deliberately to demonstrate their conviction and commitment to making the needed changes?

- Do agency leaders have plans to provide clear guidance to employees about how to conduct business during a potentially turbulent period?

Will a dedicated implementation team lead the consolidation?

- Will the implementation team have strong program management skills and a proven record of successfully working through or overseeing major transformations?

---

[2]Change management practices can be used to minimize the duration and significance of any reduced productivity and effectiveness that might occur during organizational transformations. These practices include active engaged leadership of executives at the highest possible levels; a dedicated implementation team that can be held accountable for change; and a strategy for capturing best practices, measuring progress toward the established goals of the consolidation, retaining key talent, and assessing and mitigating risk.

- Are there networks such as senior executive councils, functional teams, or cross-cutting teams that can ensure that changes are thoroughly implemented and sustained over time?

Will the implementation plan include metrics to measure progress toward the consolidation's goals?

- Will there be an action plan with goals and milestones to track progress and identify any needed mid-course adjustments?

- Will an action plan identify critical phases and the essential activities that need to be completed by and on any given date? Are there plans to publicize and report progress on specific goals for each phase of the initiative?

- Is there a strategy for tracking employee attitudes toward the consolidation and identifying any morale or productivity issues?

- Will the implementation plan include a strategy for attracting and retaining key talent?

Will the implementation plan include a strategy for assessing and mitigating risk?

- Will the implementation plan be informed by a risk assessment that includes the following five steps?

  - Set strategic goals and objectives, and determine constraints

  - Assess risks

  - Evaluate alternatives for addressing these risks

  - Select the appropriate alternatives

  - Implement the alternatives and monitor progress made and results achieved

Is there a strategy for using the consolidation experiences of other organizations and lessons learned?

- Have agency officials involved with the consolidation initiative identified and consulted with other agencies or organizations that planned for or implemented a similar consolidation effort?

- Is there a process for capturing lessons learned after each phase of the consolidation and using the information to improve the management of subsequent phases?

Appendix III: Comments from the Social Security Administration

SOCIAL SECURITY
Office of the Commissioner

May 7, 2013

Mr. Daniel Bertoni, Director
Education, Workforce, and Income Security Issues
United States Government Accountability Office
441 G. Street, NW
Washington, DC 20548

Dear Mr. Bertoni,

Thank you for the opportunity to review the draft report, "SOCIAL SECURITY
ADMINISTRATION: Long-Term Strategy Needed to Address Challenges" (GAO-13-459).
Our response to the recommendations is enclosed. We also provided technical comments
directly to your staff.

If you have any questions, please contact me at (410) 965-0520. Your staff may contact
Gary S. Hatcher, Senior Advisor for Records Management and Audit Liaison Staff, at
(410) 965-0680.

Sincerely,

Katherine Thornton
Deputy Chief of Staff

Enclosure

SOCIAL SECURITY ADMINISTRATION   BALTIMORE, MD 21235-0001

This space intentionally left blank. Pages 2-3 included technical comments that have been incorporated throughout the report, as appropriate.

RESPONSES TO THE RECOMMENDATIONS

Recommendation 1

Elevate the agency's strategic planning efforts by considering having an entity or individual dedicated to ensuring that these activities are coordinated agency-wide.

Response

We agree. We recently appointed an agency Chief Strategic Officer who reports directly to the Commissioner and is responsible for strategic planning in order to bring sustained, focused attention to long-term management challenges. The Chief Strategic Officer will ensure that the agency's strategic planning efforts are coordinated agency-wide and will keep stakeholder input at the core of our efforts.

Recommendation 2

Prepare for wide-ranging management challenges by developing a long-term strategy for service delivery.

3

Response

We agree. While our most recent service delivery plan provides detailed plans for the next 5 years and identifies service delivery options over a 6-10 year period, we recognize the need to develop a more forward looking strategy that will guide our planning and transform our service delivery to meet the needs of future customers and employees.

Our Chief Strategic Officer will lead the agency-wide effort to develop a long-range strategic plan that will integrate information technology, service delivery, and human capital plans. With the support of our leaders at the agency, we plan to build a culture that encourages and fosters strategic thinking. We expect to complete the long-range plan by February 2015 and to release it with the President's Budget for Fiscal Year 2016. We will engage with employees, advocates, Congress, and other stakeholders in the process.

In addition to embarking on a new long-range planning initiative, we are currently updating our existing Agency Strategic Plan, which spans 2013-2016. As required by the Government Performance and Results Modernization Act of 2010, our updated plan will cover the period 2014-2018. We currently have a substantial amount of engagement within our agency and with our external stakeholders. We established an Executive Steering Committee to oversee the process and have a dedicated group of skilled employees working to gather input from the public and our employees. We have asked for suggestions for innovative and efficient ways to accomplish our core mission in this environment of constrained budgets and increasing service demands. We expect to update this plan by February 2014 and to release it with the President's Budget for Fiscal Year 2015.

Recommendation 3

Mitigate the potential loss of institutional knowledge and expertise and help ensure leadership continuity by directing the Deputy Commissioner of Human Resources to update the agency's succession plan.

Response

We agree. An update of our succession plan is in the Office of Personnel work plan for calendar year 2013. In addition, in the spring of 2013, we re-implemented the national Leadership Development Program for grades GS-9 through GS-12. We plan to begin program assignments in early June 2013.

4

Recommendation 4

Determine if realigning the agency's headquarter, regional, or field office structure could yield increases in the agency's effectiveness and efficiency by launching an exploratory effort to assess the utility and feasibility of such a realignment or consolidation. These efforts could include holding discussions with other federal agencies, such as the Census Bureau and the Internal Revenue Service, to learn about their experiences undergoing similar transformations and studying the likely costs and benefits of consolidation, as well as other potential impacts.

Response

We agree. For many years, there was no alternative to face-to-face service. The Internet and the National 800 Number Network did not exist. Times have changed. The public has embraced online services. In addition to providing better service to the public, our online services save our employees time, allowing them to handle other workloads. We recognize not everyone is comfortable or able to interact with us in an automated fashion, and we will continue to work to improve this channel of public service, particularly for our most vulnerable citizens.

With workloads at an all-time high and a constrained budget environment, we will capitalize on new technologies and business concepts to cut costs, operate more efficiently, and provide the service Americans deserve. We must continue to respond to the fiscal realities, which means that we cannot do business as we always have. We have consolidated offices where it makes business sense. We know that consolidation of facilities reduces rent and overhead costs. We will begin exploring our field, regional, and headquarters organizational structures to find ways to increase our efficiency and effectiveness.

We will also initiate discussions with other Federal agencies, as suggested, to learn about their experiences with similar efforts.

5

Appendix IV: GAO Contact and Staff Acknowledgments

GAO Contact	Daniel Bertoni, Director, (202) 512-7215 or bertonid@gao.gov
Staff Acknowledgements	In addition to the individual named above, key contributions to this report were made by Jeremy Cox, Assistant Director; Isabella Johnson; Kristen Jones; and Jill Yost. Michael Alexander, James Bennett, Larry Crosland, Elizabeth Curda, Alex Galuten, Anjalique Lawrence, Steven Lozano, Elizabeth Martinez, Sheila McCoy, Adam Miles, Christie Motley, Philip Reiff, Kathleen Van Gelder, and Walter Vance also contributed to this report.

Related GAO Products

Human Capital

Social Security Administration: Service Delivery Plan Needed to Address Baby Boom Retirement Challenges. GAO-09-24. Washington, D.C.: January 9, 2009.

Human Capital: Selected Agencies Have Opportunities to Enhance Existing Succession Planning and Management Efforts. GAO-05-585. Washington, D.C.: June 30, 2005.

Human Capital: Key Principles for Effective Strategic Workforce Planning. GAO-04-39. Washington, D.C.: December 11, 2003.

Disability Program Issues

High-Risk Series: An Update. GAO-13-283. Washington, D.C.: February 14, 2013.

Modernizing SSA Disability Programs: Progress Made, but Key Efforts Warrant More Management Focus. GAO-12-420. Washington, D.C.: June 19, 2012.

Supplemental Security Income: Better Management Oversight Needed for Children's Benefits. GAO-12-497. Washington, D.C.: June 26, 2012.

Social Security Disability: Management of Disability Claims Workload Will Require Comprehensive Planning. GAO-10-667T. Washington, D.C.: April 27, 2010.

Disability Insurance: SSA Can Improve Efforts to Detect, Prevent, and Recover Overpayments. GAO-11-724. Washington, D.C.: July 27, 2011.

Information Technology

Social Security Administration: Improved Planning and Performance Measures Are Needed to Help Ensure Successful Technology Modernization. GAO-12-495. Washington, D.C.: April 26, 2012.

Physical Infrastructure

Streamlining Government: Questions to Consider When Evaluating Proposals to Consolidate Physical Infrastructure and Management Functions. GAO-12-542. Washington, D.C.: May 23, 2012.

Management Challenges

SSA's Management Challenges: Strong Leadership Needed to Turn Plans Into Timely, Meaningful Action. GAO/T-HEHS-98-113. Washington, D.C.: March 12, 1998.

Social Security Administration: Status of Achieving Key Outcomes and Addressing Major Management Challenges. GAO-01-778. Washington, D.C.: June 15, 2001.

Major Management Challenges and Program Risks: Social Security Administration. GAO-03-117. Washington, D.C.: January 1, 2003.

GAO's Mission	The Government Accountability Office, the audit, evaluation, and investigative arm of Congress, exists to support Congress in meeting its constitutional responsibilities and to help improve the performance and accountability of the federal government for the American people. GAO examines the use of public funds; evaluates federal programs and policies; and provides analyses, recommendations, and other assistance to help Congress make informed oversight, policy, and funding decisions. GAO's commitment to good government is reflected in its core values of accountability, integrity, and reliability.
Obtaining Copies of GAO Reports and Testimony	The fastest and easiest way to obtain copies of GAO documents at no cost is through GAO's website (http://www.gao.gov). Each weekday afternoon, GAO posts on its website newly released reports, testimony, and correspondence. To have GAO e-mail you a list of newly posted products, go to http://www.gao.gov and select "E-mail Updates."
Order by Phone	The price of each GAO publication reflects GAO's actual cost of production and distribution and depends on the number of pages in the publication and whether the publication is printed in color or black and white. Pricing and ordering information is posted on GAO's website, http://www.gao.gov/ordering.htm.
	Place orders by calling (202) 512-6000, toll free (866) 801-7077, or TDD (202) 512-2537.
	Orders may be paid for using American Express, Discover Card, MasterCard, Visa, check, or money order. Call for additional information.
Connect with GAO	Connect with GAO on Facebook, Flickr, Twitter, and YouTube. Subscribe to our RSS Feeds or E-mail Updates. Listen to our Podcasts. Visit GAO on the web at www.gao.gov.
To Report Fraud, Waste, and Abuse in Federal Programs	Contact: Website: http://www.gao.gov/fraudnet/fraudnet.htm E-mail: fraudnet@gao.gov Automated answering system: (800) 424-5454 or (202) 512-7470
Congressional Relations	Katherine Siggerud, Managing Director, siggerudk@gao.gov, (202) 512-4400, U.S. Government Accountability Office, 441 G Street NW, Room 7125, Washington, DC 20548
Public Affairs	Chuck Young, Managing Director, youngc1@gao.gov, (202) 512-4800 U.S. Government Accountability Office, 441 G Street NW, Room 7149 Washington, DC 20548

Please Print on Recycled Paper.